# A Night at the Beach

Diane Bair and Pamela Wright

# Contents

Rigby

A Harcourt Achieve Imprint

www.Rigby.com

1-800-531-5015

The beach looks empty, and even the kids whose parents let them stay late are home now. The fishermen have packed up their gear, and the seagulls have snatched up the last remaining bits of food spilled by beachgoers. As the sky fades from blue to purply-gray, the beach grows silent and activity ceases. Or does it?

When night falls on the beach, the magic begins. A male alligator from a nearby marsh roars into the night, hoping to attract a mate, bellowing so loudly that it can be heard a mile away. Frogs whistle a night song in nearby wetlands, and a sea turtle ends a thousand-mile journey, returning to the beach where it was hatched 20 years ago.

2

## Creatures of the Night

At night, some animals seek shelter, a place to sleep and rest, but for others, this is the time to wake up! Creatures that are most active at night are called nocturnal animals.

Most nocturnal animals can find their way in almost total darkness because they have developed powerful senses to help them to survive in the dark. Some snakes, for example, locate food by using heat sensors that help them detect small animals, such as rats and birds, that are warmer than their surroundings. Some animals, like alligators and owls, can actually see better at night.

3

We'll stay up all night tonight and visit one of the Florida Keys, which are islands off the coast of Florida. Take a closer look at the sights and sounds of the beach in late springtime, and witness the amazing things that happen on the beach at nighttime.

We arrive at the beach at dusk, when the sky is splashed with shades of red, pink, and blue, and the fiery sun is just beginning to slip beneath the horizon.

Earlier the beach was crowded with people, but now the birds have completely taken over! The sanderlings, like tiny wind-up toys, chase the waves back and forth, while nearby, a skinny-legged willet bird pecks in the sand, looking for crabs and worms.

dunes

marshland

maritime forest

mangrove

## A Home for Everyone

There's more to an ocean beach environment than sand and water—you may see windswept dunes, marshes, and freshwater rivers. There may be mangroves and maritime, or seaside, forests surrounding the beach.

Not all animals share the same environment. Some animals, such as whales, sharks, and barracudas, live deep beneath the ocean's surface, while others, like hermit crabs and shorebirds, make sandy beaches their home. Worms and tiny shrimp can be found in mudflats and tide pools. Other animals live in the dunes, marshes, freshwater rivers, woods, and lagoons surrounding the beach.

We watch as a pelican glides above the waves, looking for dinner. Suddenly, it plunges into the water, using its pouch like a net to scoop up fish. When the pelican surfaces, its pouch has expanded like a balloon, filled with seawater, and we notice a tiny silver fish wiggling in the pelican's bill. Sometimes, seagulls snatch a pelican's catch before it has a chance to swallow it, but not this time! The pelican quickly snaps its head back and gobbles the fish.

## Pelicans: High-Flying Divers

Brown pelicans are famous for their plunging dives. They can dive from as high as 60 feet above the water! Pelicans have huge, expandable pouches that can hold up to three gallons of water, and they are never far from the water, where they feed on small fish.

At one time, brown pelicans were endangered in the United States due to pesticide poisoning. Brown pelicans are now common again on the East Coast but are still listed as endangered in some parts of North America.

It's low tide, and the gooey mudflats near the lagoon are full of life. A striped snail clings to a rock. Did you know that snails release a slimy covering over their bodies when the tide goes out? This prevents them from drying up.

high tide

low tide

# What Causes the Tides?

Tides in the ocean are caused by the pull of the moon and the sun on the earth. The moon and the sun pull ocean water toward them.

High tide occurs when ocean water reaches its highest point on the coast, and this usually happens when the moon is directly over the earth. Low tide occurs when ocean water reaches its lowest point on the coast, which usually happens during a new or full moon. High and low tide happen about every 12 hours.

The longer we look in the tidal pool, the more we see. The mudflats are full of oysters and clams. Snails, oysters, and clams are mollusks, with soft bodies protected by hard outer shells.

A colony of barnacles is stuck to an empty shell—these barnacles will live on this same shell for their entire lives, not moving. Instead, they wait for the tide to wash in plankton, tiny floating creatures, for them to eat.

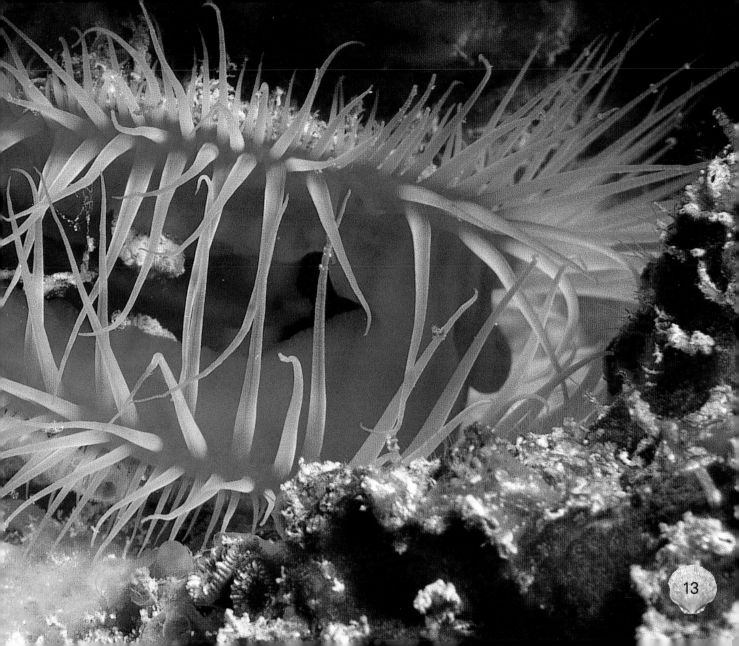

Several creatures hide in the shadows of the sand dunes, such as the gopher tortoises who crawl into underground burrows to protect themselves from predators. An eastern indigo snake slithers out of the swamp, its glossy, blue-black scales shining in the moonlight. The eastern indigo snake is the largest snake in North America and can grow to be 8 feet long. During the winter, eastern indigo snakes live in abandoned gopher tortoise burrows.

## Gopher Tortoises: Wildlife Landlords

eastern indigo snake

The gopher tortoise is a cold-blooded reptile that feeds mostly on grasses, flowers, and fruits. It averages about 10 inches long and weighs about 9 pounds. The shell of the tortoise is part of its skeleton, and it uses its shell as a hiding spot from predators when it can't make it back to its burrow.

Tortoises can live to be around 60 years old. They are a threatened species, except in Florida, where they are more plentiful. Tortoises need large areas of land, with plenty of food and room to dig burrows.

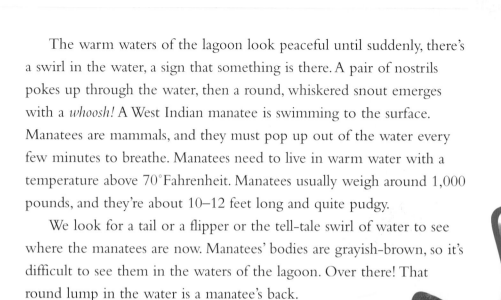

The warm waters of the lagoon look peaceful until suddenly, there's a swirl in the water, a sign that something is there. A pair of nostrils pokes up through the water, then a round, whiskered snout emerges with a *whoosh!* A West Indian manatee is swimming to the surface. Manatees are mammals, and they must pop up out of the water every few minutes to breathe. Manatees need to live in warm water with a temperature above 70° Fahrenheit. Manatees usually weigh around 1,000 pounds, and they're about 10–12 feet long and quite pudgy.

We look for a tail or a flipper or the tell-tale swirl of water to see where the manatees are now. Manatees' bodies are grayish-brown, so it's difficult to see them in the waters of the lagoon. Over there! That round lump in the water is a manatee's back.

## Disappearing Manatees

Manatees are gentle giants with no natural enemies, but sadly manatees are on the list of endangered species. Long ago manatees were hunted for their flesh, bones, and hide. Now boats are the manatee's biggest threat—speeding boats run over many manatees under the water, killing them or cutting into their backs with their propellers. Many manatees have scars on their bodies caused by accidents with boats.

Natural events can also harm manatees; when winters are unusually cold, manatees die because their bodies cannot survive long in cold water.

A short distance offshore, we see a pod, or group, of frolicking dolphins. One dolphin jumps completely out of the water as it chases a flying mullet fish, and another dolphin playfully flips its baby into the air. Dolphins are social animals who love to interact with each other. If we could see under the water, we might see the dolphins playing follow-the-leader.

18

## Bottlenose Dolphins: Water Acrobats

Watching a pod of dolphins arching their sleek bodies and jumping out of the water is a special sight. Bottlenose dolphins can jump up to 20 feet in the air and dive down more than 1,000 feet into the water.

Bottlenose dolphins grow to about 9 feet and weigh about 400 pounds. They breathe through a blowhole near the top of their head, and each dolphin has a unique whistle that never changes and is used to identify it for its entire life.

Dolphins send out various sounds and use the returning echoes to locate their prey. The dolphin can pick up sound through every inch of its skin.

What a strange sight this is! Fierce-looking creatures with spiked tails are crawling out of the lagoon. The dark, hard-shell animals look like horses' hooves, and they patrol the shallow waters, using their long tails to plow through the wet sand. These horseshoe crabs are looking for worms and mollusks.

One of the horseshoe crabs has flipped itself over, and we see its soft underbelly, a dozen legs, and a large flap. This flap hides nearly 200 gills, which the horseshoe crab uses to get oxygen from the water and air.

The horseshoe crab does not stay belly-up for long—it quickly thrusts its tail into the sand and flips back over.

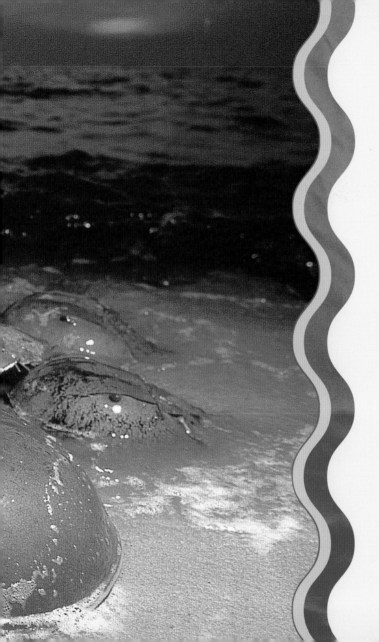

## Horseshoe Crabs: Living Fossils

Horseshoe crabs have been around for more than 300 million years, even longer than the dinosaurs. One of the reasons they have survived for so many years is their hard shells. Like many animals with shells, a horseshoe crab outgrows its shell and grows a new one, a process called molting. When it is time to molt, the old shell splits around the front edge and the crab crawls out. After 16 molts, the horseshoe crab is fully grown.

Night has fallen—inky sky meets deep purple ocean, and moonbeams cast silvery shimmers of light on rhythmic waves.

Now you see it and now you don't! It's a ghost crab—the beach phantom. It's called a ghost crab because it can vanish right before your eyes. The ghost crab moves at speeds of 10 miles per hour and can "hide" right out in the open, because their sandy-beige color blends in with the beach.

Out pops the ghost crab again, its two large black eyes sticking up. It can see so well, it can—*gulp!*—snatch an insect in midair.

ghost crab

In the distance, we hear a deep, rumbling sound that sounds like thunder but is actually the call of several male alligators.

If we got closer, we'd smell an unusual odor around the alligators, which, though odd to us, is attractive to female alligators.

## Alligators: 140 Million Years and Counting

The American alligators that live in Florida today are related to ancient reptiles that lived among the dinosaurs. Scientists have discovered skulls belonging to these extinct reptiles that are more than 6 feet long! Alligators look like large lizards, with black or gray scaly skin. An alligator has a large mouth and a strong jaw with 70 to 80 long, pointed teeth, but they don't chew or grind their food. Alligators eat all kinds of fish, birds, and mammals, and they usually swallow their meals whole!

alligators

A female loggerhead sea turtle heaves her heavy body out of the surf and onto the shore. She pushes her body over the sand with her flippers, looking for a safe place to lay eggs. She was probably hatched on this very same beach. Scientists believe that sea turtles remember the smell of the sand where they hatched and return to that place when it's their turn to lay eggs.

# Three Species of Sea Turtles

Sea turtles are among the oldest living reptiles—some sea turtle fossils are more than 150 million years old.

Seven species of sea turtles live in the world, and three of those species make their nests on the coast of Florida— the leatherback, the loggerhead, and the green sea turtle.

Leatherbacks are the largest of all sea turtles and are also the heaviest reptiles in the world. Leatherbacks can be more than 8 feet long and can weigh more than 1,000 pounds. Leatherbacks travel greater distances than any other sea turtle and also make the deepest dives.

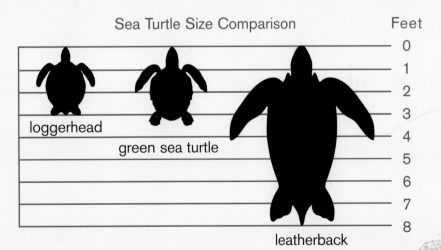

Sea Turtle Size Comparison

Feet
0
1
2
3
4
5
6
7
8

loggerhead

green sea turtle

leatherback

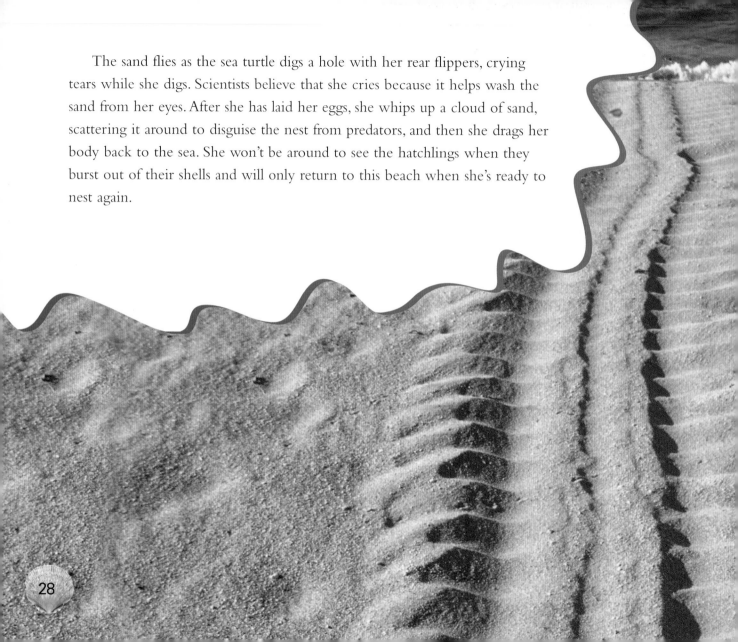

The sand flies as the sea turtle digs a hole with her rear flippers, crying tears while she digs. Scientists believe that she cries because it helps wash the sand from her eyes. After she has laid her eggs, she whips up a cloud of sand, scattering it around to disguise the nest from predators, and then she drags her body back to the sea. She won't be around to see the hatchlings when they burst out of their shells and will only return to this beach when she's ready to nest again.

## Loggerheads and Green Sea Turtles

loggerhead turtle

Loggerheads are the most common sea turtles. Loggerhead sea turtles are about 3 feet long, weigh 150 to 350 pounds, and are called loggerheads because they have large heads compared to other sea turtles. Their heads may be 10 inches wide, and they have very powerful jaws to crush food such as horseshoe crabs.

Green sea turtles have different diets than other adult sea turtles—they eat only plants. Green sea turtles are about $3\frac{1}{2}$ feet long, weigh about 300 pounds, and are named for the green color of their body fat.

green sea turtle

A raccoon scampers from its hiding place behind a patch of sea oats. Time for a snack! With the black mask of a burglar, the fearless raccoon lunges at the turtle's nest, scooping and flinging sand with its paws. Soon, tasty, fresh turtle eggs will be . . . "Scat! Get out of here!"

A park ranger and a volunteer are walking the beach, looking for turtle nests. They are fitting the nests with wire screens to protect them from predators, and tonight they arrived just in time.

The raccoon moves on, looking for an easier target. This island has plenty of food for a raccoon, mainly because raccoons eat almost anything—insects, frogs, crayfish, bird eggs, fruits, nuts, and food that people leave behind in trash barrels.

## Tumbling Turtles

What happens to the sea turtle eggs after the mother leaves the nest? In about 60 days, as many as 100 tiny turtles will wiggle out of the nest and tumble into the sand. Hatching is triggered by temperature, so sea turtles usually hatch between 11 P.M. and 2 A.M., when the sand is cool.

Then, guided by the light of the moon, they will march to the warm Atlantic surf. When they reach the water, the hatchlings paddle until they reach the Gulf Stream, swimming with the current.

loggerhead turtle hatchlings

It's daybreak and sun rays dance on the surf, bouncing light through the early morning fog.

Among the weeds, we find shells with clinging barnacles, tiny sea horses, and scurrying crabs. The high tide and strong winds have brought in many Portuguese man-of-war, which look like small balloons scattered on the beach.

## Danger: Purple Balloon on the Beach!

If you see something that looks like a purple balloon on the beach, don't pick it up! It's probably a Portuguese man-of-war, a relative of the jellyfish that can give you a nasty sting.

A Portuguese man-of-war has long feeding tentacles that can stretch up to 50 feet and are designed to sting and stun prey. Floating on the ocean, the man-of-war's soft, blue body makes it difficult to see against the water. Usually, they live far out to sea, but strong winds and currents carry them onto the beach, where they are eaten by mole crabs and ghost crabs.

Portuguese man-of-war

What else has the tide brought to shore? Several mermaid's purses are scattered among the seaweed. Mermaid's purses are cases that once contained the eggs of fish, and they got their name because they look like old-fashioned coin purses.

Thousands of coquinas, or bean clams, nestle in the sand, awaiting the next wave when the rich splash of water will provide the food and oxygen they need to survive.

Sea beans, fallen from the trees and vines in far-away places, have also washed ashore. Some people believe that sea beans are good luck.

mermaid's purses

coquinas

## Cool Beans

**Question:** When is a bean not a bean?

**Answer:** When it's a sea bean. Also known as drift seeds, sea beans are the seeds of trees and vines that grow along tropical coastlines around the world. The seeds fall from plants into major rivers and streams, eventually drifting into the ocean. Sea beans travel for miles and miles, floating with ocean currents, and finally wash up on a faraway beach.

A large black and white bird soars high in the sky, its wings stretching nearly five feet across. Its eyes are focused on the water below. It's an osprey hunting for a meal. The osprey stalls in the air, then flaps its wings before diving feet first into the water. The osprey flaps off to its nest, with the fish dangling in its talons.

Then something moving in the ocean surf catches our eye—it's a manta ray launching its massive black and white body through the water!

## Manta Rays: Underwater Gliders

Manta rays glide through the ocean like underwater birds, their wingspans reaching up to 20 feet. Manta rays are related to sharks and are one of the largest creatures in the ocean.

Manta rays have flat, broad, streamlined bodies, and some people think they look like blankets moving through the water. The name *manta* means "cloak" in Spanish. Their side fins are wide and triangle-shaped, like wings. Mantas were called "devil fish" by sailors who saw large horns extending from the fish's head. These body parts are not really horns, but scoopers, which the manta uses to guide plankton into its mouth.

manta ray

The beach may look the same as it did yesterday, but it actually changes every single day. Some changes are dramatic and happen very quickly. A hurricane can slice a channel into the land, waves can flatten sand dunes, and careless people can trample the grasses that hold the dune in place.

Other changes are slow. Over time, wind and waves are natural sculptors, reshaping an island. Here, blowing sand builds up a rippling dune. There, a foamy wave deposits a vibrant scatter of shells. The plants and animals that live on the beach are well-adapted to their ever-changing world.

Perhaps someday we'll return to this spectacular stretch of beach, but it won't be the same—it will be wild and beautiful in a different way.

# Index